SAVING YOUR FAITH, YOUR HOME, AND YOUR HOUSE:

A Guide to Faith in Turbulent Times

TOM FAY

Notice of Rights:

All rights reserved. No part of this book may be reproduced in any form or by any electronic or mechanical means including photocopy, recording, and electronic information storage and retrieval systems without permission in writing from the publisher. The only exception is by a reviewer who may quote short excerpts in a published review.

Scripture taken from the Holy Bible, NEW INTERNATIONAL VERSION®. Copyright © 1973, 1978, 1984, 2011 by Biblica, Inc. All rights reserved worldwide. Used by permission.

First Edition 2013

Second Edition 2014

Coast Publishing, Inc.

PO Box 881354
San Diego, CA 92168

info@coastpublishing.com

http://www.coastpublishing.com

Copyright © 2014 Tom Fay

All rights reserved.

ISBN: 0-9746374-7-5

ISBN-13: 978-0-9746374-7-1

THE RIGHTEOUS WILL LIVE BY FAITH

CONTENTS

	Acknowledgments	Page	i
	Introduction	Page	1
1	The Reality of Your Crisis	Page	9
2	Why Are You Doing This To Me?	Page	17
3	Just Have Faith	Page	33
4	The Definition of Faith	Page	41
5	A Depiction of Faith	Page	53
6	What Will Faith Do?	Page	67
7	Faith Will Save Everything	Page	79
8	Yes, Money Does Grow On Trees	Page	87
	Closing Thought	Page	95
	About the Author	Page	98

ACKNOWLEDGMENTS

There are so many people that I need to thank and share my gratitude. They range from Ginny who has taken jumbled thoughts, made sense of them and didn't laugh at my writing. They also include the people I bored with all my trials—and they listened. I thank my children, John and Natalie, who just kept loving me as their Dad even in the tough times. I couldn't have kept my faith without them. They are the joy of living. I thank those who read transcripts as I was formulating all my thoughts and gave me great ideas and encouragement. I also thank Theresa Janzen, my Graphic Designer, who has tremendous creative ability and skill; and helped so much to make the book more presentable. "And thanks be to God! He gives us the victory through our Lord Jesus Christ."

1 Corinthians 15:57

INTRODUCTION

The first time I was face to face with the devastation of someone losing their home was during the previous financial crisis called the Savings and Loan crisis in the 1980's. I was an elder at my church at the time, and I received a call from another elder about one of the pillars of our church.

This pillar was involved in the real estate industry and had many property investments. He and his wife were really good people. They were a loving couple married for over 25 years and by all accounts it was a happy marriage. They had blessed me on more than one occasion when we were all on a church retreat together. They seemed to practice what they believed.

He convinced some of their friends from the church to put money into their real estate investments, and at the time everyone believed real estate would always go up in price. Well, you know the rest of the story: values did not go up; they plummeted. The couple was in the process of losing their properties to foreclosure and they and their friends would lose all their capital investment.

So how does a pillar of the church handle a disastrous situation like this? Well, he and his wife covenanted together that they would go to the garage, get in their car, and run the engine until they died from carbon monoxide poisoning. That way they would not have to face their friends who they believed would surely hate them forever.

Into the car they went that fateful evening. I wonder what went through their minds as the carbon monoxide began to take effect. That God had forsaken them? How big of a failure they were? A sense of relief in not having to tell their friends they had lost all their money? Was this the way they always thought going to heaven was going to be like?

At the last minute the wife could not go through with it. She escaped the fumes. But her husband didn't. He died in the car that night, avoiding having to face the foreclosure that happened anyway.

Many reading this book have probably thought at some point that it would be easier to just leave this earth. Or those thoughts may be going through your mind even now (or you have friends that are thinking those thoughts). A financial crisis could have brought you to this point.

But it doesn't have to be just a financial crisis. There could be a myriad of events that are just as likely to be a crisis in your life. Your crisis may be the result of medical problems, mental issues, marital problems, a family, a friendship, a relationship, a drug or alcohol addiction or any number of other issues.

If you are having those suicidal thoughts now, let me assure you that there are better solutions to your problems. I've been there before and came through it. You can and will as well. In this book I will address the desperate emotions that surround foreclosure and financial failure. I also intend to give readers hope that God is in control of your foreclosure, your life, and your future success.

A personal financial catastrophe brings out the best (or worst) of us. This book addresses personal financial catastrophe in general and losing one's home to foreclosure specifically.

But the message here transcends the tough experience of foreclosure, which is just one of many types of personal catastrophes we Christians go through in life. Foreclosure is/was a national crisis affecting all people in all areas of the country, and there is evidence that Christians go through this and other catastrophes in virtually the same proportion as the rest of society.

Consequently, our churches must be full of individuals who are living from paycheck to paycheck, experiencing a loss of employment or underemployment, facing bankruptcy, approaching retirement with nothing saved, experiencing a medical issue that wiped out all of their savings, going through a divorce that is significantly lowering both spouses' standard of living, and many other life altering events.

Yes, these are the issues that we as Bible-believing, faith practicing, church attending Christians go through every day. This book is for us.

I am fortunate to have lived long enough to see the strangest things that happen in life. A friend of mine worked his whole life to build his company, sold it for $60 million, and yet ended up losing all the money. Another friend had a father who was an entrepreneur that had his highs and lows financially. His father was on top of the world one day and broke the next. His father died suddenly he when was on top, so his son, who had not worked a day in his life, was able to race Ferraris on tracks around the world and his gorgeous model wife rode show horses. When my friend's inherited money ran out his wife left him and he ended up sharing an apartment with a friend.

Life always surprises us so just know that you are not

alone in your well-laid plans going awry. The only certainty in life is that plans very seldom take the course that we want, plan, or pray about.

This book is about how we who profess to be Christians should react in those situations. I am writing in the context of a real estate foreclosure, but the same could apply to a disastrous marriage, the pain of divorce, the death of a loved one, the discovery that you have cancer or some other horrible disease, or any number of life situations that don't go as planned.

Jesus took a **sower** [1], a **king** [2], a **slave** [3], and a **leper** [4] and turned them into teaching moments about faith and the kingdom of heaven so that we could understand the lessons better.

Most people have never met a sower, a king, a slave, or a leper. But many have met someone who has lost their home and/or their house and we all have read about the millions of people in our country who have been foreclosed on over the past five years. It is because of that familiarity I am writing in the context of losing a home to foreclosure. It is my goal that through this financial crisis we too can understand the power of faith and its relevance to the

---

[1] Matthew 13:3 New King James Version
[2] Matthew 18:23 and 22:2
[3] John 8:35
[4] Matthew 26:6

SAVING YOUR FAITH, YOUR HOUSE, AND YOUR HOME:

struggles in our society.

I try to make clear that there is a difference between a home and a house. A house is made of wood, concreted, steel, glass, marble, etc. It is real estate; a piece of property. While a home is a relationship, community, love, family, memories, friendships, laughter, sorrow, sickness and health. We may have made our home within our house, but you can build a home without a house. I want to help you save both your home and your house, but the home is the far more important of the two.

I also try to relate the true experience of losing something of great value. In Chapter One I discuss the stress we go through from such a loss. I try not to minimize your feelings of stress and loss because I know from firsthand experience how real they are.

We struggle for answers, wanting to know why this is happening. It is our nature to assign a reason.

In Chapter Two I try to help you find the right reason, although I know that in many situations we never will know the answers until we see God's greater plan from heaven's perspective.

In the next six chapters I try to show that faith is the answer to our circumstances in life. I use the context of faith making mortgage payments, but faith can also heal the body, a marriage, a relationship, a ministry, provide an employment, a meal, or whatever the need is in your life.

In the last chapter I offer a final context on what you are going through in your life. It really is rather exciting, and I mean that in a good way.

I pray you will learn that God's love and wisdom is with us in the midst of everything falling apart. My great hope in writing this book is that you experience that love of God, and that you are compelled to respond by calling upon the name of Jesus, who asks us to just have faith!

I encourage you to visit my Author Page on Facebook. If you "Like" the page it is also appreciated. The Facebook page is found at www.Facebook.com/SavingYourFaith. If you enjoyed or benefited from reading this book I would also appreciate a recommendation on the Amazon page: www.amazon.com/dp/B00C100X40. This helps to spread the word of faith to many more people searching for answers.

If you have questions or would like to receive more information or if you would like me to be a speaker at your church or function I can be reached at Tom@CoastPublishing.com. Furthermore, I would love to hear your testimony of faith. I am sure many reading this book also had "miraculous" experiences because of faith.

Finally I pray for God's blessing upon your life as you "walk by faith and not by sight."

SAVING YOUR FAITH, YOUR HOUSE, AND YOUR HOME:

THE REALITY OF YOUR CRISIS

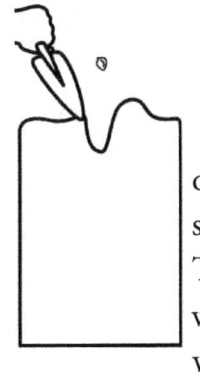

How is your sex life? (I ask the question only to get your attention.) If you are struggling financially, it's probably not great. The fact is, stress from financial difficulties will cause a lot of personal problems, of which your sex life may be the least important. Research shows that the leading causes of stress include work, lack of work, buying or losing a house, financial hardship, death, and/or the breakup of a family.

I observed that during the Savings and Loan crisis many of my real estate friends ended up in divorce. Not all, but a sad number. The stress of losing all their money was just too great to keep their family together. And remember I am using the financial crisis only as a prototype that we can relate to in the "real world." [5]

We need to avoid stress and its draining effects on our physical, spiritual, and emotional wellbeing.

Sometimes stress manifests itself in an obvious physical way such as sleeplessness, weight loss (or gain), or headaches (or migraines) and sometimes it festers just below the surface, causing an ulcer or high blood pressure. Stress may tumble you into depression. You perhaps used to have a vibrant and positive outlook, but now find yourself negative and depressed. The depression may be mild or deep. Perhaps it is bad enough that you are on prescription medication. Or maybe you are self medicating on food, alcohol, marijuana, or other mind altering drugs.

Stress affects all of our relationships including God and those we come in contact with: friends, associates, children, spouses and even strangers. You may find yourself arguing more with others either at home or work. Or you may push others away and become isolated.

Last year a friend of mine experienced the ultimate

---

[5] Your stress may have originated from some other life event; and every lesson and teaching in this book applies to your situation as well. Jesus' teaching on faith was and is a universal teaching. It applies to all of life. So when you read what I say about finances, it also applies to medical problems, relational problems, addictions and so forth.

consequence of stress. She was engaged twice to the same man and both times he rejected her prior to the ceremony and ended the relationship. According to friends this caused indescribable stress in her life. She eventually contracted a rare, chronic autoimmune disease that is thought to be the result of stress or at least aggravated by stress. Eventually it led to her death. She was a 32 year-old, beautiful young Christian woman who passed away much too early. Her story is an extreme example of the consequences of stress, but it emphasizes the deleterious effects of stress on our overall well-being. The scary part is that you may not even be aware of it.

Examples where stress has affected our mind, our bodies, our relationship with others, and most importantly our relationship with God are too numerous to recount. But you already know that and are possibly experiencing it.

Jesus knew our predicament. Even in a much less technical, slower moving, and less complicated world, he and those in his time on earth experienced stress. The people who surrounded him were worried and full of anxiety. Jesus understood that humans in their natural state worry about everything in life. One of his greatest teachings on this was in the Sermon on the Mount.

> *Therefore I tell you, do not worry about your life, what you will eat or drink; or about your body, what you will wear. Is not life more than food and the body more*

*than clothes…⁶ And why do you worry about clothes?"*⁷

Jesus explained how the lilies of the field are clothed more beautifully than King Solomon ever was.

"If that is how God clothes the grass of the field, which is here today and tomorrow is thrown in the fire, will he not much more clothe you?"

Then Jesus adds the profound comment and clue to handling stress: "O, you of little faith." [8]

Faith is the antidote for worry and stress. Jesus concludes his thoughts on worry by saying,

"Therefore do not worry about tomorrow, for tomorrow will worry about itself. Each day has enough troubles of its own." [9]

That last sentence sure is true, isn't it? Even though The Sermon was in a different context and different culture, it shows Jesus knows our stress over financial affairs in the modern world.

Paul also addressed worry, anxiety, and stress when he wrote, "Do not be *anxious* about anything." [10] Peter added:

---

[6] Matthew 6:25
[7] Matthew 6:28
[8] Matthew 6:29
[9] Matthew 6:34
[10] Philippians 4:6

"Cast all your *anxiety* on him because he cares for you."[11]

The whole Bible is full of verses on worry and anxiety, which is a real result of disconnect from our relationship with God. The Bible speaks much about fear, which is a corollary of stress; and peace, which is the absence of it. I believe it is important to know what some of those stresses look like and how they might manifest in our life. Consider if you have said or thought any of the following:

- » I am yelling a lot at my wife or husband and kids and/or co-workers
- » I don't feel like facing anyone anymore
- » My self-worth is gone
- » I can't sleep anymore
- » I wake up in hot sweats
- » I am always tired and have no energy
- » I am a failure; I'm no good; I can't do anything right
- » I don't believe there's a God and praying doesn't work
- » What is the purpose of living life anymore?

If you can relate to any of these scenarios then you are experiencing some level of stress. It is very important that

---

[11] 1 Peter 5:7

you strive to minimize stress from your life. Perhaps you can do it on your own with God's help, but if not, please seek help from others. That is not a sign of weakness, but of strength in overcoming such extreme hardship.

Underlying the stress from not being able to provide for our family's needs is the stress between God and us. I know that even we as Christians hide our true feelings in order to be acceptable. Men do this instinctively and then add to that the pressure to look acceptable to those sitting next to us in Church. Add to that the expectations of being good Christians we have doubled the stress! We mouth, "God will provide," but worry even as we say the words.

The actual and potential damage from stress can linger when unchecked for years. It is like a virus. As an example, if you had chickenpox as a child the virus is still in your body and the potential for developing shingles later in life still exists. Similarly, unresolved issues may persist years after losing your home. They need to be addressed now so that they don't fester and become pain later or even a total disaster. The loss in equity you built up in your house will do years of damage to your retirement. But the loss of family, friends, and trust in God does many more years of damage to us.

Yes, in our natural human state there are plenty of things to worry over and be anxious about. But Jesus showed us the antidote to being a worrisome human and that is living a life of faith. Through faith we can move the mountains of doubt and debt we have accumulated and the stress burying us.

It is important to rid ourselves of that stress because it destroys too many things. God empathizes with us through His Son, Jesus, who is there to help us and save us as we put our faith in him.

SAVING YOUR FAITH, YOUR HOUSE, AND YOUR HOME:

GOD, WHY ARE YOU DOING THIS TO ME?

I have had the pleasure (or excitement or stupidity) of being in the middle of the ocean for twelve days while sailing 1,000 miles through the Bermuda Triangle on a small 26-foot sailboat with my son. The waves were 9 to 15 feet high and very rough for the first four days. Between that, the rain, and lightening, I prayed a lot. When in a big sea of debt, we also tend to reach out to God and pray a lot for help. As a Christian you certainly have prayed about your financial situation (or other adversity in your life). I know I do.

I am sure you have asked the question: "Why are you doing this, God?" Is the financial trouble we are in the result of something we did or didn't do and is God is punishing or disciplining us? Let's take a closer look at that question and see if we can shed some light on it.

But before I get into a more theological discussion of why things happen in the spiritual life of a believer, let's consider first the more real world aspect of why. If you signed a loan document that had a monthly loan payment of $3,000 that covered principle, interest, taxes, and insurance per month and your take home pay had only been $3,500 for the last several years, then you are in financial trouble because of an unwise thing you did.

If you smoked cigarettes since you were a teenager and now have cancer, you are in pain and are facing daily death because of a lifestyle choice. If you are in jail because you killed someone while driving home drunk, your freedoms and opportunities have been stripped from you because of a reckless decision you made. If you have been diagnosed with Type 2 Diabetes because of obesity, you made a lot of stupid decisions in not exercising or eating a proper diet.

You are not the first irresponsible person in the world nor will you be the last. But it is the perfect time to heed the words of Jesus to repent. [12] Repentance is "to change one's *way of life* as the result of a complete change of thought and attitude." [13] The consequences may or may

---

[12] Mark 6:12

[13] Biblical Repentance/The Meaning of Repentance, By L.R. Shelton Jr. About Repentance Chapter 2 of the book Biblical Repentance

not already be set but repentance and living a life of faith is certainly the antidote for stupidity. [14]

But stupidity, recklessness, irresponsibility, or a lack of wisdom is not always the reason we end up in very difficult situations. It comforts our soul and renews our spirit to discover that hardship can be an opportunity to do God's work. This is the first step to eliminating the stress in our life and beginning to live a life of faith. Repentance is the first step if we caused the problem all by ourselves.

Our prayers originate from a number of different perspectives. One of the first is simply a cry for help! And then the questions follow: *Why? What did I do wrong? What was my sin?* The questions arise from the belief that our behavior dictates what happens in our lives. And surely there are adequate verses in the Bible that support this viewpoint:

"Do not be deceived: God cannot be mocked. A man reaps what he sows." [15]

"Remember this: Whoever sows sparingly will also reap sparingly, and whoever sows generously will also reap generously." [16]

---

[14] Please accept my personal apology for being blunt but truthful. My desire is not to diminish you but to call you to action.
[15] Galatians 6:7
[16] Corinthians 9:6

So we either did not sow enough of the good or right things or we sowed some sinful act.

Proverbs is also full of such teachings:

My son, do not forget my teaching,
　　but keep my commands in your heart,
for they will prolong your life many years
　　and bring you peace and prosperity. [17]

Honor the Lord with your wealth,
　　with the first fruits of all your crops;
then your barns will be filled to overflowing,
　　and your vats will brim over with new wine. [18]

Those who give to the poor will lack nothing,
　　but those who close their eyes to them
receive many curses. [19]

And in Malachi:

Bring the whole tithe into the storehouse, that there may be food in my house. Test me in this," says the Lord Almighty, "and see if I will not throw open the floodgates of heaven and pour out so much blessing that there will not be room enough to store it. [20]

---

[17] Proverbs 3:1-2
[18] Proverbs 3:9-10
[19] Proverbs 28:27
[20] Malachi 3:10

You may have given graciously to the Lord expecting God to not only return the gift to you, but to multiply it many times over. You may have given to God because someone said that you would receive many blessing back in return for your gift. Or you believed one or all of the verses above. You honestly believed that the Spirit spoke to you and told you to give to someone or some ministry. Yet here you are today, not only without the blessing, but without the seed as well.

But as soon as we think there is a formula that allows us to manipulate God for our benefit, he proves us wrong.

What caused your financial problem? Do you know? I've listed a few things to help jog your memory and stir your heart so that the real issues can be brought to light. Once they are then you can deal with them.

» I committed a sin.

» I didn't tithe.

» I was not surrendered and I am being punished.

» God has forsaken me because I forsook him.

» God doesn't care – I don't feel his love anymore because I didn't care.

» I had an affair and God is taking away my home.

» I was a workaholic and didn't have time for God.

> - I forget to pray and be thankful and I think God has forgotten me.

> - I lied on my loan application so I am losing my home because of that.

> - I used money for vacation that I should have given to the church.

> - I committed an unspeakable sin.

You may have done one or more of the things above and that is the reason that God is allowing these things to come into your life. However, you may have done one of those things and God is not punishing you for your action; but instead it appears that God is actually blessing you richly.

In this chapter I want to tell you the answer to the question of why God is doing these things and why these hardships and catastrophes are happening to you. Someone may have already told you why things are not going well for you. Usually their reasons are not so good for your self-esteem. Frequently, your friends will tell you the reason God is allowing these things to happen is to teach you something.

Read the entire book of Job sometime and see how friends can say the cruelest things. Here is just a small selection from "The Message Bible" [21] of Eliphaz' explanation of why Job lost his home and had other bad things happen to him:

> *Do you think it's because he cares about your purity*
> *   that he's disciplining you, putting you on the spot?*
>
> *Hardly! It's because you're a first-class moral failure,*
> *   because there's no end to your sins.*
>
> *When people came to you for help,*
> *   you took the shirts off their backs, exploited their helplessness.*
>
> *You wouldn't so much as give a drink to the thirsty,*
> *   or food, not even a scrap, to the hungry.*
>
> *And there you sat, strong and honored by everyone,*
> *   surrounded by immense wealth!*
>
> *You turned poor widows away from your door;*
> *   heartless, you crushed orphans.*
>
> *Now you're the one trapped in terror, paralyzed by fear.*
> *   Suddenly the tables have turned!*
>
> *How do you like living in the dark, sightless,*
> *   up to your neck in flood waters?* [22]

---

[21] Eugene Peterson, The Message Bible: NavPress Publishing Group; Colorado Springs; 2002
[22] Job 22:3–11

I've had people tell me some harsh things so I know how Job felt but hopefully your friends haven't been that cruel.

But as a Christian you've probably heard the reason for your lack of financial success was because of something you did; some sin you committed. In fact, this is the most common reason we give ourselves: We think that God is either punishing us for a sin we committed or that he is disciplining us for errors of our ways that needed correction.

This belief has been around since the inception of human thought. Early cultures often attributed floods, fires, droughts, or any natural disaster as a punishment by the gods. Those societies concocted all sorts of ways to appease the angry gods, including human sacrifice.

During the time of Jesus it was also a common belief that bad luck was actually the consequence of sin. Jesus gives two examples of bad things that happened to people and asks the crowd if that happened because of their sin. Listen to what he says,

> *Now there were some present at that time who told Jesus about the Galileans whose blood Pilate had mixed with their sacrifices. Jesus answered, "Do you think that these Galileans were worse sinners than all the other Galileans because they suffered this way? I tell you, no! But unless you repent, you too will all perish.*

> *Or those eighteen who died when the tower in Siloam fell on them—do you think they were more guilty than all the others living in Jerusalem? I tell you, no! But unless you repent, you too will all perish.* [23]

Jesus is saying that the degree of sin was not borne out in greater punishment; in fact, that suffering and catastrophe that happened to these men in these two situations is not the consequence of their greater sin. He then warns us that we will perish unless we repent.

There is another account in John where the disciples ask Jesus if a man's blindness was the result of sin.

> *As he went along, he saw a man blind from birth. His disciples asked him, "Rabbi, who sinned—this man or his parents that he was born blind?"*
>
> *"Neither this man nor his parents sinned," said Jesus, "but this happened so that the works of God might be displayed in him."* [24]

Have you considered that maybe your calamity is not the result of your sin, but is happening so that the works of God might be displayed through you to the world? It is very possible and maybe even probable. So do all that you can so that God will be glorified. It's not easy or even

---

[23] Luke 13:4
[24] John 9:1–3

graspable perhaps at this moment, but try to imagine that it is actually a blessing that this catastrophe has come into your life and that through you God is doing wonderful things in this world.

I like the response of the blind man that Jesus used as an example in the passage above. "'Lord, I believe,' and he worshiped him." [25]

So you see, this concept of bad things happening to people because of sins that they've committed has been around a long time but is debunked by Jesus.

You may be relieved that all those sins you committed have not culminated in this disaster. That takes a lot of guilt off your shoulders. But sin in a Christian's life is not pleasing to God and he does discipline us to help us get rid of that sin and cause us to lead a life of faith instead.

If this catastrophe is the result of our sin and/or lack of faith then this discipline that God is performing in our life should also be a comfort to us because it is a sign that he loves us. The author of Hebrews explains this concept most eloquently:

My son, do not make light of the Lord's discipline,
and do not lose heart when he rebukes you,

---

[25] John 9:38

> *because the Lord disciplines the one he loves,*
> *and he chastens everyone he accepts as his son.* [26]

So let's put this in perspective. First, I explained that the present hardship may not be the result of sin, but of some greater plan God has for us and/or other believers in this world. Now I am saying that if it was because of a sin then God is disciplining us because he loves us. So what is the answer to the question of this chapter — God, why are you doing this to me? Is it because of my sin? — *maybe* or *maybe not*.

Hebrews again puts this into perspective:

God disciplines us for our good, in order that we may share in his holiness. No discipline seems pleasant at the time, but painful. Later on, however, it produces a harvest of righteousness and peace for those who have been trained by it. [27]

And even if God is using this for his glory, I am not sure it makes the pain less painful, but it does bring us closer to God. On the one hand it increases our faith and gratitude for all the blessings we have received. On the other hand it brings us to a greater love and closeness with

---

[26] Hebrews 12:5
[27] Hebrews 12:10b–11

Him because we have been disciplined and are casting away our sin and this is pleasing to God.

To summarize:

» There is no formula that manipulates God to give us blessings and happiness. Furthermore, it's a sin if we do try to make him prove himself to us in some way.

» Feelings that you are responsible for your situation because of a sin you committed may not be the case at all. We have seen that bad things happening in our life are not in direct correlation to our acts of sin.

» That said, God does discipline us so we'll live by faith and shake off the sin habit that may be a hindrance to His glory.

» In either case, what David said makes a lot of sense: "Search me, God, and know my heart; test me and know my anxious thoughts." [28] This search of our hearts is an extremely valuable activity on a daily basis and I would encourage it.

» Let me also make it clear that the blessings you may have in your life today — and lack of stress — may or may not be the result of your righteous living

---

[28] Psalm 139:23

and generous giving. We ought not seek to live a righteous life so that we can receive a lot of material things of this world.

» Whichever situation, God is in control. In the one situation he is bringing these things into your life for your good. In the other, you are part of a much bigger plan to bring glory to God. How can we complain about that? In fact we might even say, "God, if you have more, bring it on!"

There is no sugar coating the trials, anxiety, turmoil, heartache, and tension you are going through. But God is treating you in love and is so very concerned about you and the details of your life—where you will live and what you will eat and how you will clothe yourself. We don't see it when we are going through it but, unbelievably, this is the best of life.

Really? The best of life?

Yes, this is the best because God loving us and taking care of us is really as good as it gets, isn't it? And that is the reason James is able to say, *"Consider it pure joy, my brothers and sisters, whenever you face trials of many kinds."* [29]

---

[29] James 1:2

So consider these times with pure joy. There is another verse I have that I want to share: *"Weeping may stay for the night, but rejoicing comes in the morning."* [30]

And Psalm 126:

Those who go out weeping,

carrying seed to sow,

will return with songs of joy,

carrying sheaves with them. [31]

However, all of this takes faith, doesn't it? How else could we be calm in the storm? That is what this book is about: the faith to save your home and your house.

In conclusion I apologize if I have burst the bubble of many Christians who see God as the supplier of all their wants who will make life wonderful for them. Sorry, but there is no magic formula [32] that manipulates God and forces him to give us a good life filled with joys and toys

---

[30] Psalm 30:5

[31] Psalm 126:6

[32] Just ask the godly Christian martyrs, who were tortured for their faith and gave the ultimate sacrifice of their lives because they would not deny the Lord and Savior they love — ask them if there is a formula to make you happy and richly blessed materially.

and things that make us happy and successful. Trying to manipulate God is pretty frustrating and fruitless so those practicing a formula eventually will see the futility of trying to be in control.

"The righteous will live by faith." [33]

---

[33] Habakkuk 2:4; Romans 1:17; Galatians 3:11; Hebrews 10:38

SAVING YOUR FAITH, YOUR HOUSE, AND YOUR HOME:

JUST HAVE FAITH!

The way to save your home from foreclosure (or whatever the turmoil is in your life) is to just have faith. At least that is what Jesus says:

"If you believe, you will receive whatever you ask for in prayer." [34]

"And I will do whatever you ask in my name, so that the Father may be glorified in the Son. You may ask me for anything in my name, and I will do it." [35]

"And so that whatever you ask in my name the Father will give you." [36]

---

[34] Matthew 21:22
[35] John 14:13–14
[36] John 15:16

Whether it's having food, clothing, shelter, health, casting out of demons, or whatever—Jesus' answer was to have faith.

So Jesus is clearly placing the ability and power to change our physical environment in our capacity to have faith in him. Moving a mountain of dirt or a mountain of debt, what's the difference? I think the debt would be easier. But faith will move both.

"If you have faith as small as a mustard seed, you can say to this mountain, 'Move from here to there,' and it will move. Nothing will be impossible for you." [37]

Moving mountains is not the only thing that faith accomplished. Whether Jesus directly says, "Your faith has healed you;" or if it is the implied message, faith was the common denominator throughout the entire ministry of Jesus. Everything, and I mean everything, was a result of faith. Let's look at some of the direct connections:

» The two blind men that followed him calling out: "Have mercy on us, Son of David!" When Jesus saw their faith, "Then he touched their eyes and said, 'According to **your faith** let it be done to you.'" [38]

» The Canaanite woman with the demon possessed

---

[37] Matthew 17:20
[38] Matthew 9:27-29

daughter: "Then Jesus said to her, 'Woman, you have **great faith!** Your request is granted.' And her daughter was healed at that moment." [39]

» The paralyzed man who was lowered through the ceiling by his friends: "When Jesus saw their **faith**, he said to the paralyzed man, 'Son, your sins are forgiven.'" [40]

» The woman who had been subject to bleeding for twelve years and just touched his cloak: "He said to her, 'Daughter, **your faith** has healed you. Go in peace and be freed from your suffering.'" [41]

» The sinful woman who washed Jesus' feet with her tears: "Jesus said to the woman, '**Your faith** has saved you; go in peace.'" [42]

» Raising the daughter of Jairus, a synagogue leader, from the dead: "Hearing this, Jesus said to Jairus, 'Don't be afraid; **just believe**, and she will be healed.'" [43]

» The Samaritan leper that was healed: "Then he

---

[39] Matthew 15:21–28
[40] Mark 2:1–5
[41] Mark 5:25–34
[42] Luke 7:36–50
[43] Luke 8:40–53

said to him, 'Rise and go; **your faith** has made you well.'" [44]

» The blind beggar who received his sight: "Jesus said to him, 'Receive your sight; **your faith** has healed you.'" [45]

After reading through the above instances where faith changed life's circumstances, do you now begin to understand that faith will also change your life's circumstances? Faith in God's ability and power can move that mountain of debt. Our Christian faith believes that God can also make mortgage payments. We are of a belief that divine intervention is initiated by faith because the inspired scripture that we hold to for faith and practice says it is so. We believe that God created the heavens and the earth and that he still controls the elements, whether the dirt of the mountain; gold or paper in the bank; or the water of the sea.

When Jesus walked on water it became as solid and firm as the ground we stand on. How did he do that? Faith!

"Lord, if it's you," Peter replied, "tell me to come to you on the water." "Come," he said. Then Peter got down out of the boat, walked on the water, and came toward Jesus. But when he saw the wind, he was

---

[44] Luke 17:11–19
[45] Luke 18:35–43

afraid and, beginning to sink, cried out, "Lord, save me!" Immediately Jesus reached out his hand and caught him. "You of little faith," he said, "why did you doubt?" [46]

In each case Jesus makes the point that it was their faith and God's mercy and power in response to their faith, which caused the change in their circumstances.

But let's go one step further: without faith there was no healing, casting out of demons, or miracles of any sort. Jesus personally experienced this in his hometown when those who knew him as a child could not put their faith in him.

"And he did not do many miracles there because of their lack of faith." [47]

Let's put this in perspective again. You have a mountain of debt that you are unable to pay. Maybe your house is worth much less than the mortgage on it. Perhaps your credit cards are loaded. You have problems! If you could solve those issues by yourself you wouldn't be reading this book; they would already be solved. But your problems are like most in the Bible — they are beyond a human's ability to solve.

---

[46] Matthew 14:28
[47] Matthew 13:58

The miracles that Jesus performed when he healed, cured, fed, or raised to life all had faith as the foundation. So it stands to reason that if all you have is debt, faith surely must be the answer.

And because you are reading this book, it is probably because you have already exhausted all of your options and faith and luck are left. And luck has already turned against you and is running away like an Olympic gold medalist.

When faith is the only solution left, God has you right where he wants you. This is a good thing. And this might be an appropriate time to thank God for leading you to this point in your life.

To those who have no debt, but are reading to learn more about faith, your only viable option is to live the best life God has for you. It is foolish to think you can escape God's ability to control the affairs of your life. I know you know that, but let me remind you of the parable of the Rich Fool. [48]

And he told them this parable: "The ground of a certain rich man yielded an abundant harvest. He thought to himself, 'What shall I do? I have no place to store my crops.'

Then he said, 'This is what I'll do. I will tear down my

---

[48] Luke 12:16–21

barns and build bigger ones, and there I will store my surplus grain. And I'll say to myself, 'You have plenty of grain laid up for many years. Take life easy; eat, drink and be merry.'

But God said to him, "You fool! This very night your life will be demanded from you. Then who will get what you have prepared for yourself?"

This is how it will be with whoever stores up things for themselves but is not rich toward God. [49]

God intervenes in our life and just as he has blessed those who are financially poor and live in poverty, he has also blessed others with a full barn. It is up to both the poor and the rich to look and to trust God for everything He has blessed us with.

This is the reason James says:

Now listen, you who say, "Today or tomorrow we will go to this or that city, spend a year there, carry on business, and make money." Why, you do not even know what will happen tomorrow. What is your life? You are a mist that appears for a little while and then vanishes. Instead, you ought to say, "If it is the Lord's will, we will live and do this or that." As it is, you boast in your arrogant schemes. All such boasting is

---

[49] ibid

evil. If anyone, then, knows the good they ought to do and doesn't do it, it is sin for them. [50]

As a Christian we are to trust God for all our daily needs. So, yes, God is very much involved in where you live. As one who has trusted in God for your eternal salvation I say to you, even though you might have considered other paths, faith is the answer to your every provision.

So whether your barns are full and you have a wonderful life, or your pantry is bare and you don't know where you will lay your head, have faith in the God who loves you.

---

[50] James 4:13–17

THE DEFINITION OF FAITH

So what is this faith that pays mortgages?

Our churches teach "the faith." That is called doctrine. But that is not the faith I am talking about. I am talking about faith as an action.

Faith is not easy to practice. It demands action on our part to practice and produces action on God's part as a result. These two forms of action are very powerful. For Christians who do not practice faith, who are practicing unbelief, their experience is much easier to perform on a daily basis. That makes their Christianity a religion or legalism.

The problem with religion and legalism is that

they remove us from God and they are a heresy of true Christianity. Jesus came for the purpose of debunking the efficacy of the law (even though he fulfilled it) and replacing it with a new covenant of grace and the power of faith operating in the spiritual Kingdom of God. On top of that, religion and legalism just aren't fun or joyful or fulfilling, and they don't work to bring us closer to God.

There are many definitions of faith, but let's look at the one from Hebrews.

"Faith is the substance of things hoped for, the evidence of things not seen." [51]

That's a good definition, and it becomes even clearer as you read the entire chapter of Hebrews 11, which is known as the faith chapter of the Bible.

The author of Hebrews who writes this widely quoted definition of faith uses two real estate terms. The first term is translated in the New International Version of the Bible as "substance." This was a real estate term that was used by the Greeks to describe the foundation or cornerstone of a building. That is faith: the solid rock foundation upon which we can build our life and the entire relationship with God.

It's ironic that the foundation and substance that we

---

[51] Hebrews 11:1

are to have faith in is related to a house, one that you may be in peril of losing. But faith is the firm and trusted foundation as opposed to a worldly foundation that is built on shifting sand. [52]

The second word is translated "conviction," as in "conviction of things not seen." This word was used by the Greeks to denote a deed to a property. So there are two ways to know if you own a house. The first is if you take possession of it and live in it. The second is when you leave your home but still own it because you have a deed. Even if you rent it out to another family and they have possession, everyone else knows that you are the owner because you have the deed. Faith is that sure. Faith is carrying that deed in your pocket.

But there is obviously a much deeper meaning in the words foundation and deed. This meaning got lost in the Bible translations when Martin Luther translated it. His associate, Melanchthon, said it should be translated in such a way that it took on a more individualistic meaning. And indeed, the reformation was all about an individualistic faith in contrast to a communal faith of the church. An individual relationship with God was the correct approach, but is not quite what this verse is trying to say. So Martin Luther gave it a meaning like "faith is *my* assurance of things hoped for, *my* conviction of things

---

[52] Matthew 7:26

not seen." And ever since Martin Luther, Protestants have translated the passage that way. But for the 1,500 years before Luther, translators adopted a different perspective within the context of Hebrews 1:3 and 3:14.

The first passage says:

"The Son is the radiance of God's glory and the exact representation of his being." [53]

So faith also is the exact representation of what we hope for. Notice the difference in how Martin Luther translated the word versus how the scholars who came before him. Faith is not us being sure; rather, it is the exact representation of what we expect. This reality is in none other than God himself as revealed in the person of Jesus Christ.

Remember when Jesus said:

"If you have seen me, you have seen the Father." [54]

Just like the real estate term foundation is the exact representation of the floor plan of the house, so faith is exactly what it is you expect or anticipate. Faith is not a wish or a hope and a prayer. Faith is the reality.

This hope is much larger than you hoping and praying

---

[53] Hebrews 1:3
[54] John 14:9

for a house, car, refrigerator, iPad, new clothes, or your health. This hope is for sure the entire—past, present and future—relationship with God for all eternity. The rest of the chapter bears this out. [55]

When you put your faith in Jesus Christ's death and resurrection for your sin you are also putting your faith in all that God will do for you throughout eternity. That means there is no parenthesis—where you must take control over your life—between your born again experience and your living eternally with God. Faith is the complete and total reality that your sins are forgiven, your needs are provided and your eternity with God is assured.

Think of the absurdity if we came to God at our new birth and said, "God I trust Jesus' work on the cross for my salvation and believe that I will be with you for eternity, but for the rest of my days on earth I can handle everything myself." How ridiculous that is. So faith is the substance of all we hope for—from salvation to eternity—with no interlude where we take over.

The second half of the first verse—"certain of what

---

[55] "All these people were still living by faith when they died. They did not receive the things promised; they only saw them and welcomed them from a distance, admitting that they were foreigners and strangers on earth. Therefore God is not ashamed to be called their God, for he has prepared a city for them. "Hebrews 11:13–16 partial.

we do not see"—makes more sense now, too. I think there is an even better translation of the word *certain* and that is *proof*. So faith is the *proof* of what we do not see. If you have the deed to your home, then you have the proof that you own it even if you are not in your home at that very moment.

You cannot visually see or perhaps even comprehend that you will live with God for eternity except that you believe—have faith—that you will. That faith is the proof you will live with God for eternity. How do you know your sins are forgiven? You have faith. Faith is that proof. Faith is that deed you carry with you that says your sins are forgiven. And how is it that you know God will provide for your needs this day? Faith is the proof. Faith is that evidence of all things that are not seen. Faith is the proof that God will provide your food, clothing, shelter and peace in your heart today.

There is an amazing verse at the end of the faith chapter in Hebrews. It is verse two of chapter 12:

Looking unto Jesus the author and finisher of our faith; who for the joy that was set before him endured the cross, despising the shame, and is set down at the right hand of the throne of God. [56]

---

[56] Hebrews 12:2

The word author was used by the Greeks to denote the hero who founded a city and thus gave it a name. For example, Athena was the author of Athens. She was the one who gave Athens its meaning. So Jesus is the author of our faith. It is not something that we conjure up on our own; it is not where if we just think and pray enough we will get God to do something for us. It is there because Jesus authored it and let us in on it.

He also is the perfecter, the one who brought faith to its completion and wholeness. He also practiced faith to the very end. And for that reason he is sitting on the right hand of God's throne. As we practice faith till the very end, we too will have an eternal place prepared by God.

Let me paraphrase verse 2 of chapter 12.

Looking unto Jesus the author and finisher of our faith; who for the joy that was set before him endured the foreclosure, despising the shame, and is set down at the right hand of the throne of God in a really wonderful home.

So just as faith gave Jesus the perfect place for him to live at the right hand of God, so also faith will give us a really wonderful place to live and have our home!

As we have seen Hebrews 11:1 is talking less about what an individual is feeling or thinking and more about the reality as found in God. So as a Christian if you are given the choice between trusting yourself, a friend or God, we definitely would pick God. Friends can be rather flaky or human, even the best of them at times. Or if we are given a choice between trusting in the things of the world or God, we would have to choose God.

The world is corrupt, failing constantly, going to war for unwarranted reason, deceptive, etc. The world is also a bit slimy, filled with selfishness, ego, lies, and even worse.

So when we are given the choice between choosing the world or God, God wins every time. And that is what the author is saying: faith is the reality; all else is a shadow (without any substance).

I always thought that if something was unseen then it wasn't real. But no, since we have the deed, although we are on a vacation and not seeing our home, we still own it. Faith is the reality so in our time of need we must live by faith.

Don't assume that one can sit around doing nothing and wait for all these things to fall from the sky. That will not happen. It didn't happen in Jesus' day, Paul's day, or our day. But it was with faith that all these things were provided to them.

There was an occasion when Jesus and the disciples needed money to pay the temple tax. It was provided miraculously: Jesus had Peter go to the lake and cast out a line. The first fish he caught had a four-drachma coin in it—the exact amount of the tax. The money for the tax didn't fall from heaven—Peter had to the lake, get his fishing equipment, and go about his fishing activity—but it was still heavenly provided. [57]

In the next chapter I will be giving a more in-depth description of what faith is, but I want to conclude this chapter with a biblical illustration.

Exodus 16 tells how and what the children of Israel ate in the desert after they departed from Egypt. As you recall, they began to grumble because they had no food and wished they were back in Egypt where at least they could die in their homes with full stomachs. We look down at them now, but in reality we are not much different from them. Here is God doing some great event in our lives—like he did in theirs, freeing them from slavery—and we grumble that things are not going right. And yes, they had hardship and lost their comfortable homes in Egypt. But God was leading them to a better place—a promise land.

So God provides them bread from heaven, literally. Every morning they went out and found "thin flakes like frost" [58] on the ground. They were told to collect it, but only enough that would feed them for that one day. They

---

[57] Matthew 17:24–27
[58] Exodus 16:13

called this bread manna. [59]

Some people, though, collected more than one day's ration. They did not trust God to feed them the next day. Well, what they didn't eat that day, "was full of maggots and began to smell" [60] the next. But on Friday morning they were to collect two days of provision because God didn't want them to work on the Sabbath. Again, some doubted God and went out on the Sabbath to collect for that day – and there was none to be found. But what was collected on Friday for two days was fine on the second day but was only good on the Sabbath.

Let's put this in perspective: every single day for forty years until they entered the Promised Land, they had to trust God to feed them. But in fact, we too are called to trust in God each day for our daily bread. As Jesus taught his disciples to pray:

"Give us this day our daily bread" [61]

As expressed in Hebrews 11:1, faith was the reality; it was proof they would live and thrive. Faith was the exact representation of their daily provision; faith was the proof they would be fed. That act of faith generated a miraculous

---

[59] Exodus 16:31
[60] Exodus 16:20
[61] Luke 11:3

event for them each day. And there was the action of them collecting enough manna for just that day; it came from God, but they still had to collect it.

That is what faith is and does. Faith will change the circumstances of your life too.

SAVING YOUR FAITH, YOUR HOUSE, AND YOUR HOME:

A DEPICTION OF FAITH

In the previous chapter I shared how God defines faith. Too often we stop at the definition as if that bit of knowledge does anything to help us out of a situation like foreclosure. Now let's look at faith in action a step further, but based on the static definition of faith. Let's go back to Hebrews 11. After the definition in verse one the author says in verse two:

"By faith we understand that the universe was formed at God's command, so that what is seen was not made out of what was visible." [62]

Why does the author say that? Is he teaching

---

[62] Hebrews 11:3

creationism? No, he is not making a scientific statement but rather a theological statement. In order to have faith one must first—and I stress *first*—have the knowledge of God and must believe that God has the ability to perform that which you are asking him to perform.

If God can create the universe then he can save my home from foreclosure.

This is a condition logic statement. If the one statement is true, then the other must be true also. When you pray the Lord's Prayer and ask him to "give us this day our daily bread" you must first believe that he has the ability to actually provide it to you. We preface that request with "Father, hallowed be your name." [63] If God has all the power to create the universe, then he has the ability to provide bread to me this day (and clothing and shelter).

So first, faith is your action of placing a total and complete dependence in God who has the power to perform and accomplish that activity to which you are requesting. In other words, He can do it! The emphasis here is He. One thing you will find is that God does not like to share the spotlight. In the Second Commandment God says:

---

[63] Luke 11:2

"For I, the Lord your God, am a jealous God." [64]

Whenever there are too many cooks in the kitchen it is always God that leaves the kitchen first—immediately. God does not share this activity with anyone because he is a jealous God. We believe and he delivers. In other words, if we plan on helping God, then God leaves the task to us, and he leaves. This is hard to understand and practice. We even have a saying in our culture, "God helps those who help themselves." But nothing could be further from the truth. In fact, God does not help us when we try to do God's work. We are to do our work and he will do his. He gives us this day our daily bread; and we believe (have faith) that he will.

Let's look at Job again since he lost all his income and homes and had extreme medical and relational crises. When God finally answers Job after he has lost virtually every possession and his entire family, does the Lord God say to Job how sorry he is for putting Job through all those hardships or that he was tested because he was such a godly man? And that he is so proud that Job did not deny him? Is there an emotional side to God where he feels sympathy for all of Job's pain and suffering and loss? No, not one bit. He says to Job:

---

[64] Exodus 20:5

> *Brace yourself like a man;*
> *I will question you,*
> *and you shall answer me.*
>
> *Where were you when I laid the earth's foundation?*
> *Tell me, if you understand.*
> *Who marked off its dimensions? Surely you know!*
> *Who stretched a measuring line across it?*
> *On what were its footings set,*
> *or who laid its cornerstone—*
> *while the morning stars sang together*
> *and all the angels shouted for joy?*
>
> *Who shut up the sea behind doors*
> *when it burst forth from the womb,*
> *when I made the clouds its garment*
> *and wrapped it in thick darkness,*
> *when I fixed limits for it*
> *and set its doors and bars in place,*
> *when I said, 'This far you may come and no farther;*
> *here is where your proud waves halt'?* [65]

Job gets no credit for his godly life or good deeds done. And why should he? Neither do we. And why should we? God is the creator of the universe. He laid the earth's foundation and has the absolute discretion to do anything He wants. We are not here to help Him; He helps us.

---

[65] Job 38:3–11

Martin Luther ushered in the reformation when he taught that salvation is by faith and faith alone. Martin Luther read what Paul said:

"For it is by grace you have been saved, through faith — and this is not from yourselves, it is the gift of God — not by works, so that no one can boast." [66]

We tend to understand fairly well that salvation is a work that God performs by himself as a result of faith. But once we are saved, why do we no longer need to trust God? We feel we must help him, even though helping God for salvation is not something that we really consider (at least in evangelical theology).

Non-believers try to help God all the time. They think that if they do enough good works God will reward them by accepting them into heaven. All they need is 51 percent good deeds to 49 percent bad deeds. For salvation we believe that we are sinners and that there is a great gulf between God and us because of our sin. And that Jesus Christ died on the cross and rose again for our sins. And if we believe we will be saved.

"For God so loved the world that he gave his one and only Son, that whoever believes in him shall not perish but have eternal life." [67]

---

[66] Ephesians 2:8–9
[67] John 3:16

So if your life has been trying to help God, you should not be too hard on yourself. Even the converts attending the churches founded by the apostle Paul had this same problem with mixing works and living by faith. From the Message Bible:

Answer this question: Does the God who lavishly provides you with his own presence, his Holy Spirit, working things in your lives you could never do for yourselves, does he do these things because of your strenuous moral striving or because you trust him to do them in you? Don't these things happen among you just as they happened with Abraham? He believed God, and that act of belief was turned into a life that was right with God. [68]

So you see, human nature is to help God out, to give him a hand. But it never works. It will backfire, so stop it. He really doesn't really need your help, nor does he want it.

So what we have then is this: first, with faith we understand and acquiesce that God has the power and ability to perform; second, we must relinquish the undertaking to perform on our own. If we don't think he can perform or if we think we can help him perform, then he won't perform at all.

Let me give you an example from Matthew's gospel

---

[68] Galatians 3:5–6

account. [69] In Capernaum, a Roman centurion, or army officer, came to Jesus and asked him to heal his servant who was paralyzed and suffering terribly. The centurion was not a Jew but Jesus offered to go to his home and heal the servant. But the centurion refused.

"Lord, I do not deserve to have you come under my roof." [70]

Remember the point I made that we have nothing to offer God? The centurion understood that. He felt totally unworthy. But the centurion fully understood the power and the ability that Jesus had. For he says to Jesus:

"For I myself am a man under authority, with soldiers under me. I tell this one, 'Go' and he goes; and that one, 'Come.' And he comes. I say to my servant, 'Do this,' and he does it." [71]

The centurion fully understood that all Jesus had to do was to give the command to the universe and his servant would be healed. God has the ability to order someone or something to come and it comes. God can say, "Do this" and it will be done. God can say, "Stall the foreclosure" and it will be stalled.

---

[69] Matthew 8:5–13
[70] Matthew 8:8
[71] Matthew 8:9

The centurion had faith that Jesus could and would heal his servant. And Jesus said to those around him:

"I have not found anyone in Israel with such great faith."[72]

Someone once said, "Let God be God." God does have the power and not only does he not need us, he does not want us messing around in his working.

Why would God not want us to help him? By doing so he would have to share glory. And this is one thing God does not like to do. Sharing glory with God is akin to making us mini-me gods. And that never sits well with the almighty God. The angel Lucifer tried that once and it didn't go over very big then either.

So it is this: God can and only God can.

One of the reasons we must keep ourselves out of God's business is that we have nothing to offer God. Money? He has far more, plus he can take yours away anytime he wants, but you cannot take his away. Good works? I doubt it, but in fact you have a lot of nasty works too and God has only good works. What do you really have to offer to God that he lacks? We really have nothing. If anything, we get in his way.

Therefore if you have nothing to offer to God, there is

---

[72] Matthew 8:10

nothing that you can dictate, demand, or expect him to do. All we can do is have faith. I like to call it *unconditional faith*. It is that type of faith that puts no "strings" on God. There are no conditions that you put on him. There is just the unconditional faith (that raw belief that is displayed in the relinquishing of ourselves and the embracing of who he is and what he has done) that he loves you and will provide for you.

All we can do is come to God knowing that *"It's impossible to please God apart from faith."* [73] And why? Because anyone who wants to approach God must believe both that he exists and that he has the loving power to respond to those who seek him.

We find it easy to espouse faith for our salvation, but we find it so hard to accept it into our daily way of life. We come up with terms and concepts that have no measurement or meaning other than man's comparison to each other: such as "walk in the Spirit," "surrender," "Spirit filled," "dedicated," "more committed," "give your life," etc. And we run as fast and far as we can from the most fundamental, radical, revolutionary covenant that God made with man — unconditional faith.

You may want your home to come out of foreclosure so you can stay there comfortably, but he may want you

---

[73] Hebrews 11:6

in a larger or smaller one and he may have a new family that he wants to put into your home. If you demand him to do a particular thing it may actually be against both your good and his greater good.

This should not discourage you because even though we cannot put expectations on God, he does make certain promises to us that are really quite thrilling. We can expect our actions of faith will be of benefit to us. Paul makes it clear that "all things work together for good." [74]

Yes, what God will do as a result of our faith will be to our benefit. It will be good for us. It will not disappoint. We can expect that good to be now or later in this world, or later after we die and are with him in eternity. What difference does timing make if indeed what God does is to his benefit and ours? I am happy with that because it really is rather good.

It is at this position of us having nothing to offer that God intervenes and reacts in miraculous ways; and those ways are typically different from our expectations.

That does not mean you should quit your job to stay home and pray, having faith and trusting God to provide food, clothing, and shelter. The response of faith does not imply doing nothing. In fact, it is quite the opposite.

---

[74] Romans 8:28

Paul founded the church in Thessalonica on one of his missionary journeys, and said to them not to have anything to do with those who are lazy. If your current situation is the result of being lazy, I don't think faith is what you need; you need to repent and change your ways.

Keep away from every believer who is idle and disruptive and does not live according to the teaching you received from us. For you yourselves know how you ought to follow our example. We were not idle when we were with you, nor did we eat anyone's food without paying for it. On the contrary, we worked night and day, laboring and toiling so that we would not be a burden to any of you. [75]

Let me give you some examples of faith in action that produced miracles. Remember the men who carried their crippled friend to get healed?

Some men came carrying a paralyzed man on a mat and tried to take him into the house to lay him before Jesus. When they could not find a way to do this because of the crowd, they went up on the roof and lowered him on his mat through the tiles into the middle of the crowd, right in front of Jesus.

When Jesus saw their faith, he said, "Friend, your sins are forgiven.

---

[75] 2 Thessalonians 3:6–8

Did they just sit by believing that Jesus would find them? No, they tried every conceivable way to reach Jesus, but the crowd was too large and wouldn't let them in. Finally they went to the roof, carrying him up there, removing the tiles and then figured out a way to lower him down in front of Jesus. Do you think they carried rope with them? I doubt it. I think they encountered problem after problem getting their friend in front of Jesus. And did you ever think about what the homeowner thought when his roof had a hole in it? Do you think they just said to him, "Have faith"? I don't think so, sometimes faith is a lot of effort and activity, although not a burden. But it is not doing God's job; it is doing our job.

I want to close this chapter on a very short note, but with a mental picture that tells it all. It is from the wise King Solomon. He says:

"The horse is made ready for the day of battle, but victory rests with the Lord." [76]

You can picture this in your mind: all the preparation of feeding, watering, exercising, and training the horse, then saddling and into battle you go, slugging it out with the enemy. But the victor in battle rests with the Lord. So too with your foreclosure or whatever catastrophe you

---

[76] Proverbs 21:31

are encountering now. Fight the battle with everything you have, which is never quite enough. But in the end, it is the Lord that brings about victory through your faith.

Every day and throughout the day when going about your activities of work, fun, or saving your home and house, trust in God to provide all these things for you. Have faith. Have faith in him giving you victory. It is his battle. It is yours to win through faith.

SAVING YOUR FAITH, YOUR HOUSE, AND YOUR HOME:

WHAT WILL FAITH DO?

Faith as described in the previous chapter produces miracles. Let me clarify what I mean by a miracle. The dictionary says that a miracle is "an event that is contrary to the established laws of nature and attributed to a supernatural cause." [77] What I mean by a miracle then is that God (the "supernatural cause") intervenes in the normal course of world or human events, in time, and rearranges the events.

Let me explain this a bit further by referencing a very strange healing recorded by Mark:

---

[77] miracle. Dictionary.com. Collins English Dictionary - Complete & Unabridged 10th Edition. HarperCollins Publishers. http://dictionary.reference.com/browse/miracle (accessed: October 31, 2012).

> *They came to Bethsaida, and some people brought a blind man and begged Jesus to touch him. He took the blind man by the hand and led him outside the village. When he had spit on the man's eyes and put his hands on him, Jesus asked, "Do you see anything?"*
>
> *He looked up and said, "I see people; they look like trees walking around."*
>
> *Once more Jesus put his hands on the man's eyes. Then his eyes were opened, his sight was restored, and he saw everything clearly. Jesus sent him home, saying, "Don't even go into the village."* [78]

There are a couple of things that are hard to understand here. The first is why Jesus used his saliva to heal the man and the second is why it took Jesus two times to touch him before he could see accurately.

I am not going to solve those issues, but I do want to point out that the man was not healed by an instant implant of something or strange tissue or anything like that. He was healed by all of the cells of the man's eyes and brain working properly. There is nothing unusual or miraculous about eyes working properly, other than the miracle of sight itself but there is something miraculous when God intervenes in the man's life and rearranges the cells including the speeding up in time the creation

---

[78] Mark 8:22-26

of new cells that work properly. Note: there is nothing unusual about the creation of cells, either; but it is the time in which they were created or generated that makes it a miracle. Someday we may see this as commonplace: A blind man goes to the hospital and stem cells create the correct cells and neural connections for him to see. But Jesus accelerates the stem cell action so that it is an immediate healing. God is not bound by time.

So it is with the miracles that are produced by faith. It is not that faith causes God to bring in a new element from another dimension; it is that God takes the existing and rearranges it and/or speeds up or reverses time so that the event or physical situation is changed.

Let me give you another example of what I mean. Jesus said:

> *Truly I tell you, if you have faith and do not doubt, not only can you do what was done to the fig tree, but also you can say to this mountain, "Go, throw yourself into the sea," and it will be done.* [79]

We tend to think that it is quite miraculous to move an entire mountain into the sea.

However, we know that eventually the mountain will go into the sea. Over time rain and weather will erode

---

[79] Matthew 21:21

the mountain and the water will take it into the sea. The Appalachian Mountains used to be like the Rocky Mountains, but time has eroded them.

So the miracle is not so much the event itself, but it is the rearranging of events and the intervening in time, which God also created and controls. Let's take a look at your situation. Lets say that you don't have the money to make a house payment or credit card payment. It is not that you will never have the money, because at some point you will have a job that will give you the money that could have made the payment.

So faith inspires God to intervene in the affairs of the world and rearrange the events or matter. This rearrangement may be where he speeds up the money you would make in the future and brings it to the present; or he rearranges the money in society and takes some from the rich and gives it to the needy—you.

There is an illustration of Jesus rearranging nature when he turned the water into wine at the wedding in Cana, his first miracle. [80] Jesus had the servants fill six stone water jars each containing twenty to thirty gallons with water. When the servants tasted the water, they discovered it was actually the best wine at the wedding. Yes it was a miracle. But it was also God rearranging the

---

[80] John 2:1-11

time and events. Everyone knows that it takes water to nourish the grape vines to produce the fruit. God entered into the time and events of growing grapes and creating fine wine and he rearranged those events to miraculously produce the wine in the way only he can do and just like he will rearrange the affairs of your life.

That is what faith does. And what a beautiful thing it is. Faith pleases God to provide for our daily needs. God delights in your faith. Faith is his design and He loves to see you live your life in faith and trust in him for all your needs. He loves to reward those who live their life by faith. He loves to take the burden off our shoulders and give us peace. Faith is the catalyst between God and man.

Let me talk for a moment about non-faith. The religious philosophy that God exists but doesn't intervene in the affairs of the world is known as deism. The illustration used is that of winding a clock and then just letting it go and run by itself. Deism claims that God wound up the universe and then left it to run all by itself according to the laws of nature.

Many of the founding fathers of our nation had a theology of deism. Therefore, you have a lot of references to God in their writing, but the deist has no expectation of God intervening in world affairs. They could look backwards and see God, but would not believe that he came into the world during the present and caused a change.

Deism is not a Christian theology. Yet practically speaking, many Christians seem to live their life in a deistic manner. Some say that Christ came into the world 2000 years ago and sacrificed his blood for our sins, crediting that past event for their salvation. But they don't see any more miracles happening in their life. They see no reason to live by faith, which to them is a theology but not something that causes the almighty God to intervene in life and cause the miraculous to happen.

Christianity says that God is constantly and continually active in the world's affairs. This means that God actually is concerned about your foreclosure or crisis. He does care about where you are going to live and how you will take care of your family.

I would like to relate two personal stories to you from my own life. During the Savings and Loan Crisis of the 1980's I had a very nice home in the suburbs. I was involved in the real estate industry and like everyone else had borrowed heavily from some Savings and Loans for my real estate projects. But when the crisis came I ran out of cash. I was very active in my church at the time; God was using my ministry and me. I had given cheerfully and faithfully. I felt I was in the exact place I was supposed to be.

I prayed continually about my situation and yes, I believed that God would save me from financial ruin. I believed it with my whole heart. But guess what? I lost everything material and a lot, lot more.

What did that do to my faith since I had really prayed in faith and trusted God? Well, it didn't destroy it, but at the time it sure made me wonder about a lot of things, probably just as you are wondering about all the things happening now.

Now, let me tell you a story about another home I had after losing the one described above. In the late 1990s-early 2000s I ended up with an even nicer home. I had lived there for about fifteen years. I was able to buy it because someone else lost it. God worked that out.

But a few years before the current crisis started I fell behind on my payments. Again I just didn't have the cash flow and went a few months without making mortgage payments. I got the typical letters from the lender, then the attorney, and then I received a courtesy call from the lender's attorney saying that they were going to file all the foreclosure papers on that Friday. I had until then to bring my loan current. After that the process was very swift and certain that I would be homeless.

At that time I also had a business in the Bahamas (yes, the pain and suffering). I mention this because I will never forget that morning (before that Friday) that I walked Cable Beach thinking about every possible way

I could come up with the payments I owed. I thought about what I could sell, earn, pawn, ~~steal~~, or whatever. There were some options there, but not very good ones.

I had walked to the pier and sat down contemplating all those options. Then I thought that I needed a "backstop" if they all failed. A backstop in business or life is the "Plan B" that if all else fails there is that one last option that will work.

When I was going through my financial troubles in the Savings and Loan crisis I had a friend — my best friend — that said to me one day, "Tom, I know you are going through really difficult times and I want you to know that I am your friend and I will give you whatever you need." I did have to go to him several times and without asking a single question he wrote out a check for the few thousand I needed.

So I thought as a last resort he would help me again if I needed and asked. I told myself, "Yes, that is my backstop."

At that instant I felt reprimanded at saying that a human being was my backstop. I apologized to God and said in my heart, "God is my backstop." In other words, at the very last resort, if all else failed in my work efforts, God was my backstop.

That is when faith took over. It was at that moment that I allowed God to do the miraculous. He became my backstop.

Let me explain that concept a bit more. I didn't walk back home rejoicing that my house was saved and that money would fall out of heaven. I still continued to work very hard, tried to sell anything I could and checked out the pawnshops. I didn't stop those activities, but every time I got anxious and worried—which was a lot—I kept thinking and believing that God was my backstop.

It is there, at that point when we know in our hearts that God has both the power and the desire to take care of our situation that he then performs the miraculous. And remember, the miraculous is often different from what we think it will be.

Now let's go back to my situation. Did money fall from heaven? No. Was my anxiety over? No. But the strangest thing happened. Remember the lawyer that called me and said that she was going to file all the foreclosure papers on Friday? Well, she lost the file and/or forgot to file the foreclosure. Somehow it disappeared from her To Do list. In fact, she lost it for 19 months.

Think about it though—every day for 19 months I am thinking about and worried my home is going to be foreclosed on that day. That is a lot of worry. And every day I have to have faith that God will take care of me and be my backstop. And every day I hear nothing from the bank or the lawyer. The bank continued to make the real estate tax and the property insurance payments, but never sent me an invoice for my monthly payments anymore. This goes on for 19 months.

And during those 19 months I was able to raise money by selling something. Once I had the money in hand I called my lawyer to contact the bank's attorney and work out the payments. The bank did charge me, though, for *one* late payment.

If God did the miracle exactly as we want or expect, it wouldn't be a miracle from God. You see, God is not a servant; he is a sovereign. He decides how he wants to do things. He does them his way and not ours.

> *"For my thoughts are not your thoughts, neither are your ways my ways," declares the Lord.* [81]

To continue the story, have I ever worried since? Yes, of course; all the time. But now I know something for sure. If God could save my home that way, he can do anything. It is like I have an anchor that cannot blow me away. And it has been that knowledge that has been a life changing experience for me. I am so thankful that you are going through these horrific times so that God will teach you the same.

---

[81] Isaiah 55:8

"Consider it pure joy… whenever you face trials of various kinds." [82]

---

[82] James 1:2

SAVING YOUR FAITH, YOUR HOUSE, AND YOUR HOME:

FAITH WILL SAVE EVERYTHING

That experience of God saving my home in a miraculous way anchored my faith. The storms of the world can blow, Satan can bluster, and the lusts and desires of the world can look so tempting, but I now have an anchor of faith that holds so very strong.

I compare this anchor to the United States landing a man on the moon. How many times have you heard or said, "If we can put a man on the moon, why can't we make …"

To me that experience became the turning point in my life, where "If God can hide a file from an attorney for 19 months and makes her forget it, then he can…" Yes he can do anything I need.

I think every believer needs an anchor; that one event of faith that is so monumental and miraculous that we continually refer back to it as an example of both what God can do and what happens when we put our faith in the almighty God.

In 2008 I had the opportunity to convey this concept of an anchor to a friend of mine. We were in business together and having an incredibly profitable year. We were building and importing mopeds/scooters manufactured in China and selling them to dealers throughout the United States. They were really high quality and the dealers we had understood the value. This was in contrast to many other China made scooters, which were being imported into the country illegally; something the Environmental Protection Agency (EPA) knew about it and was trying to crack down on.

Our company had four containers of scooters at the US port and one of them was selected by the US Customs Department to be opened and inspected. Unbeknownst to us, on that particular container of scooters an employee in China who made the EPA label typed the letter "N" rather than "M" on the EPA plate.

So when Customs looked up the EPA license they couldn't find it and all four containers were confiscated as illegal. We also had 22 more containers that were on the water from China and all of them would be confiscated as well. That would not only have bankrupt and destroyed our company and personal finances, it would have also destroyed all the relationships we had built up in China.

Needless to say, it was a very stressful time. My friend and business partner was especially in turmoil because he had invested years of his life into the enterprise and now in a matter of days and weeks it could all come crumbling down.

For me, I was still basking in what had happened a few years before and was convinced that for God this was an easier task than hiding a file.

I told my friend about the anchor concept and assured him that this was going to be *his* anchor. When God solved this small problem then he too would have an anchor that would carry him through life's storms.

My friend had been raised in a Christian family and was a church leader so faith was not unheard of for him. But it was only a concept and not something that actually caused the almighty God to intervene in the world and cause people to do or not do certain things.

As the negotiations with the government dragged on, my friend's emotions and mind experienced more and more anguish.

Just as I had tried for 19 months to save my home, we

tried everything to solve this EPA problem. We frequently talked about the anchor and how God would use this for both of us. It was hard for him to understand, but I had an anchor, so it was much easier for me. I had no idea how we would get out of this situation, but I knew God knew.

Finally, one day my friend gave the problem to God alone. "Okay God, it is yours. I give it to you. I believe you have the ability and desire to solve this problem. I believe that is what you will do because I have nothing that I can offer except my faith in you."

At that very moment two things happened. First, a great burden lifted off his shoulders. The world is a heavy burden to lift but faith is not a burden. Jesus said:

"Take my yoke upon you and learn from me, for I am gentle and humble in heart, and you will find rest for your souls." [83]

The second thing that happened within minutes of my friend putting his complete faith in God was the government called to tell me they were going to release our containers. Obviously we had to change the EPA plates, but we could do that in our own warehouse with our own staff.

---

[83] Matthew 11:29

Not long after getting off the phone my friend came into my office to announce he was trusting God to take care of it. He was relaxed and happy even though he had no idea the government had just called. When I told him his first reaction was disbelief. Next, we both were overcome with humility, joy, happiness, and amazement.

He called the staff together, who would have all lost their jobs, and told them the good news. He got down on his knees and said we need to pray and thank God. Before he bowed his head, he looked over at me and said, "I have an anchor now."

Since that day we have seen so many more examples of God doing the miraculous at our work. We still spend endless hours in planning, working, selling, filling out forms, and doing accounting. We have had our faith tried on many other occasions but we always come back to the fact that we have an anchor that is our faith. "If God can work out the affairs of the United States Federal bureaucracy, he can…"

Perhaps you have an anchor. Maybe you call it something else. Or maybe you are about to get an anchor. Wouldn't that be exciting! When you put this financial event into perspective and meditate about God using it to teach you some glorious lesson and experience faith, it is awesome!

In closing this chapter I don't want to leave the impression that faith or an anchor of faith is some magic potion that makes us successful and happy all the time. For as we see in Hebrews 11, many:

> *"through faith conquered kingdoms, administered justice, and gained what was promised."* [84]

And yet...

> *There were others who were tortured... Some faced jeers and flogging, and even chains and imprisonment. They were put to death by stoning; they were sawed in two; they were killed by the sword. They went about in sheepskins and goatskins, destitute, persecuted and mistreated – the world was not worthy of them. They wandered in deserts and mountains, living in caves and in holes in the ground.* [85]

But the key to understanding the role of faith is this: faith is the only mechanism that gives us the peace and joy in our heart and the closeness to our loving God. So whether we are, by faith, conquering kingdoms or

---

[84] Hebrews 11:33
[85] Hebrews 11:35-38

wandering destitute and being mistreated; we have peace, "which transcends all understanding," [86] and joy in our hearts, and we grow closer to our loving God. Does anything get better than that?!

---

[86] Philippians 4:7

SAVING YOUR FAITH, YOUR HOUSE, AND YOUR HOME:

A GUIDE TO FAITH IN TURBULENT TIMES

8

YES, MONEY DOES GROW ON TREES

Now be honest: How many times have you condescendingly asked your child, or maybe your spouse, "Do you think money grows on trees?" Or maybe someone asks you that. Annoying, isn't it?

What they really mean is, "I don't have the money to buy that for you."

What if money actually did grow on trees? When you needed a new pair of Nike's or an iPad or even a better car, you could simply go into the back yard and pick enough ripe $100 bills and go buy it. No work involved; just the effort to reach up and pluck the money off the tree.

The currency in the kingdom of this world is the dollar. But in the kingdom of God, which Jesus introduced to us and taught during his three years of ministry, the currency is faith. So with the currency of faith, people do all the normal things that occur in the seen world: they buy bread[87], pay their taxes[88], receive their healthcare[89], and experience happiness[90]—all the things that they would do otherwise in the world. The difference is that in God's kingdom He provides food, clothing, and shelter in a much better fashion than the world does; he also gives us peace within our hearts, lightens our burden, and takes away worry and anxiety.

It is in this context of God providing all things for us through the currency of faith that I say money *does* grow on trees. Let's look at two instances in the gospels when Jesus seemingly created more than $22,000[91] out of thin air.

The first is in Mark 6:30-44 when Jesus feeds the five thousand and the disciples picked up twelve baskets of

---

[87] Mark 8:1-10
[88] Matthew 17:27
[89] Mark 5:25-34
[90] Philippians 4:7
[91] According to the IRS, the national average wage index for 2011 is $42,979.61. http://www.ssa.gov/oact/cola/AWI.html. More than half a years wages would then be around $22,000.

leftovers. The second is in Mark 8 [92] and he feeds four thousand. This time he had seven loaves of bread and yet they picked up seven baskets of leftovers.

That really is quite miraculous. It really is the equivalent of picking $22,000 off the money tree. If I had been there those days, I would have said, "I have an anchor now."

How did these loaves multiply? I don't understand everything but I do know two things. First, a kernel of wheat has the ability to reproduce itself many fold. And second, God is not bound by time. To me it was indeed a miracle; God intervening in the world, rearranging time and events, and changing the natural outcome.

When Jesus taught his disciples to pray "give us this day our daily bread," I believe he was envisioning these miracles; that God would intervene in the natural course of events and provide for our food like he did for the five thousand and the four thousand.

You may say you have a job and can buy what you need without God. It is true that many do this. The unbeliever works and buys his bread. The difference is that when we do it with faith, we have the load taken off our shoulders,

---

[92] Mark 8:1-9

have joy put in our hearts, and praise God because he did the miraculous in our midst.

Jesus explains how this miraculous provision works in greater detail in Mark 4:26 in what is known as the Parable of the Growing Seed:

> *He also said, "This is what the kingdom of God is like. A man scatters seed on the ground. Night and day, whether he sleeps or gets up, the seed sprouts and grows, though he does not know how. All by itself the soil produces grain—first the stalk, then the head, then the full kernel in the head. As soon as the grain is ripe, he puts the sickle to it, because the harvest has come.*

Jesus tells us exactly what he is trying to communicate in this parable. His description is not the kingdom of the world; we know what that is like. [93] That is a kingdom of slavery to so many things: money, greed, lust, etc., of heavy burden, of worry and anxiety. Instead, He tells us what the kingdom of God is like.

---

[93] Galatians 5:19-21: "The acts of the flesh are obvious: sexual immorality, impurity and debauchery; idolatry and witchcraft; hatred, discord, jealousy, fits of rage, selfish ambition, dissensions, factions and envy; drunkenness, orgies, and the like."

And come to find out, in the kingdom of God money does grow on trees. Well, it is actually closer to the stalk of wheat. In his kingdom we go about our jobs, sow the seed, and then harvest the crop. But it is God that does everything in between those two events. How does that seed know when to sprout? How does it know to send the root down to absorb the soil nutrients, and how does it know to send the leaf up to absorb the sun's rays, and who taught it photosynthesis?

Jesus tells a parable about a farmer planting wheat, but it applies to us today. We don't know how he takes care of us, but when we have faith in him God produces a commodity — wheat, money — out of nowhere.

Just in case the disciples didn't fully understand he related another parable, this one called the Parable of the Mustard Seed. He describes the mustard seed as the smallest on earth, his point being that just by looking at the seed there is nothing to indicate it will grow into a tree where birds can rest. That is like faith in the kingdom of God. There is no way you can see with your eyes all that God is doing to provide shelter for you. He may be creating money to make your payments, or he may be moving a family out of their home to make room for you. You don't know how this works or what the Father is doing, but it is by faith that we know it happens.

So how do you make the house payment when you don't have the cash, the currency of the world? You use the currency of the kingdom of God, faith, to save your *home*.

It just may be that you can use the faith currency to save your house, too. That's what I used when I needed to save my houses from foreclosure. In one case he moved me out and ended up giving me a better one. In the other he performed a miracle that kept me in my house.

Both moving and staying in my houses were God's will that brought glory to Him in this world. They were anxious times for me and filled with struggles, but faith overcame that anxiety and peace filled my being each day, as I trusted him.[94] And you, too, are now being blessed with this opportunity to put your complete trust in God as he provides you with food, clothing, and shelter. Does it get any better than that, whether you have to move *or* stay?

---

[94] I want to add a further personal note. Many mornings I would wake up at 3:00 or 4:00 AM in a sweat from worry. I couldn't go back to sleep so I got in the habit of reading the Bible. I actually started in Genesis 1:1 and would read as long as it would take me to find strength and faith for that day. Sometimes I could find it in a few verses but other days I would have to read chapters. And just like the manna from heaven, it lasted only one day. The next morning it would repeat itself and again I would read the scriptures until I found enough strength for that day. I also kept a journal of what God taught me. And looking back, those were the best of days

We can now pray this prayer:

*Now to him who is able to do immeasurably more
    than all we ask or imagine,
according to his power that is at work within us,
    to him be glory in the church and in Christ Jesus
throughout all generations, forever and ever! Amen.* [95]

---

[95] Ephesians 3:20

SAVING YOUR FAITH, YOUR HOUSE, AND YOUR HOME:

CLOSING THOUGHT

"In the beginning God created the heavens and the earth." [96]

My personal belief is that angels love coming to earth because it's a wonderful amazement for them. Here in one small corner of the universe is a planet teaming with life, a rare, special and unique event. The angels must love to see it.

The angels must also love to see God's grace and mercy; to see God provide the miraculous and do wondrous works. On the night Jesus was born, a single angel announced to the shepherds that Christ the Lord was born in Bethlehem. Multitudes of angels wanted to observe this event also.

---

[96] Genesis 1:1

> *"Suddenly a great company of the heavenly host appeared with the angel, praising God."* [97]

The same was evident at the end of Jesus' life. He said:

> *"Do you think I cannot call on my Father, and he will at once put at my disposal more than twelve legions of angels?"* [98]

They were there at his crucifixion to see God's amazing grace. And they were there at his resurrection to roll the stone away from the grave. [99]

It is my personal belief there are many angels here waiting and watching to see the miraculous events that are going to happen when you put your faith in Jesus Christ to provide for your food, clothing, shelter, and well being. It is not just for our selfish needs that God provides, but also for the entire universe to rejoice. You may feel like all is going to hell but in reality all is coming from heaven.

Rejoice now with the multitude that is waiting for your exercise of faith to activate God's power, grace, and love. The angels will love it, just as you will. Does your life get any better than that???

---

[97] Luke 2:13
[98] Matthew 26:53
[99] Matthew 28:2-7

ABOUT THE AUTHOR

Where does one start in describing Tom Fay? Probably the best place is the passion of his Christian faith and serving God in ministry. Yet for 35 years he has been out of the "full-time" ministry and been an active entrepreneur in the business world. In the business world he was a real estate developer, a telecommunications consultant, a technology innovator, a business development consultant, and an Internet marketer. In these activities as a typical entrepreneur he made and lost several multimillion dollar fortunes. So being on top of the world was not an unusual event for him — and neither were the low times of having nothing.

In his youth he was the founder of the Southern California Bible College which merged with a seminary to become Southern California Seminary. He served as Senior Pastor of the Fletcher Hills Bible Church. He was also a publisher of the first line of humorous Christian Greeting Cards.

Tom Fay graduated with a Diploma in Theology from the Grand Rapids School of the Bible and Music, now Cornerstone University. He also graduated from Simpson University with a Bachelor Degree in Psychology. Currently he is earning his Masters of Arts Degree at Fuller Seminary.

He is the father of two wonderful children and resides alone in San Diego, California. He can be reached via email at Tom@CoastPublishing.com.

www.ingramcontent.com/pod-product-compliance
Lightning Source LLC
Chambersburg PA
CBHW071304040426
42444CB00009B/1869